# NOW THE WORLD TAKES THESE BREATHS

# NOW THE WORLD TAKES THESE BREATHS

## JOAN METELERKAMP

modjaji books

Acknowledgements
Three of these poems appeared with translations into
Portuguese by Golgona Anghel in Proximo Futuro/Next Future,
October 2013. Thanks to Golgona and to the Fundacao Calouste
Gulbenkian for this, and for the opportunity of reading these
poems at the "Festival of Literature and Thought of Southern
Africa" in June 2013.
Eight poems were first published in *New Coin*.

Published in 2014 by Modjaji Books
PO Box 385, Athlone, 7760, Cape Town, South Africa
www.modjajibooks.co.za

ISBN 978-1-920590-53-6

Cover artwork by Tammy Griffin
Cover lettering by Carla Kreuser
Author photograph: Jenny Metelerkamp
Book and cover layout by Danielle Clough
Printed and bound by Megadigital, Cape Town

For Frances and Dominic
and Paul and Michael

# Contents

Coruscating cold
corrosive     excoriating cold
snow-so-they-closed-the-airport-on-Christmas-night cold
four-sleety-lanes-of-traffic-each-way-vertiginous cold
        vertiginous verges
            sickly lit
                tunnel of underground traffic
                tiled   like a lavatory

stinking subway
        filthy snow slit-
        eyed  sun-tilt
cold so I couldn't stand up in it
                            straight
cold.

I thought: get me out of this hell cold
and I will kneel down to the ground;
*Do It*, said the plumber, a total stranger
at home. *Give Thanks, Give it Up*, taking the line
of least resistance. I slipped out to give
the dogs water, didn't watch my back,
lifted – forgot to bend my knees – twisted!
It felt like *this will hurt me as much as
it hurts you*, punishment for wickedness
I wasn't aware of, not strong enough
to pick up a bucket!
        So much for prayer,
granted, but the body, the unseen
muscles of the bending back, resisted.

What did I think – I hadn't really lost her?
*Wake up! For crying out loud open your eyes,*
said the thick wind, the light alive like through rock
pools (or my mother's greeny-brown eyes);
who would have thought Kempton Park
so close to O. R. Tambo with all its shitty little brick
buildings we cruised over and in, in
the night, half past   four in the morning

after no sleep at all after all dream like light!
I mean   recognized:
not that our daughter
wasn't happy, I knew
that, I realised, but
so far the other side!

That side, there, we walked the *Freedom Trail*:
death everywhere; even the light, frail,
round the corner, Lewis Wharf, where *dear friend*
*you cannot change* Bishop wrote of Lowell,
O *Quaker Grave-yard*, O little bowed over angels
in all the city's little burial-
patches, between imperial red-brick riches
stone-slab grey hunched against the wet;

(but hot air breathing egregiously out of invisible orifices
between the glass panels of the *Holocaust Memorial*) O *Kaddish*.

In Concord, where it started, the Resistance: black ice;
*Little Women*   you who nursed   mercury in the blood
*poet of the body and poet of the soul*
this isn't what I thought to write!

Dry, seedy summer when we returned,
bees under the cupboard floor-boards,
musty smell of sweating   wax   or was it   the honey
smelling of shoes in closed cupboards;

deadly poisonous boomslang cruising the *dombeya*, the wild-pear;
weeds everywhere;   fleas, mosquitoes breeding like mosquitoes
in the cesspool-reservoir-pool;   blocked loos;
at last the plumber came     blocked the passage;   stood there
with what we used to call verbal diarrhea logorrhea
going on and on about God till I could hardly stand it
matter not mattering! The plumber! Get through it! Shit! Shit
in the old outlets, hot water geyser completely clogged;

my back seized: lay down on my son's empty bed, hauled
my body to the old brown couch where he used to lie, cried.

Bent back and the internal wail...*aaay!*
wasting your days on your dry hill
like an eighty four year old
father's dutiful daughter – fucking hell
even the plumber has the answers!
*You Have Come Back from the Other Side*
*Be In It*   whatever that is   *Everything's a Sign.*
Graffiti on the pavement outside the petrol station   *WHY*
why what?   You O Lord?   Even the old earth goddess gave up
everything she'd given birth to that's how the Mysteries began!
Easy explanations – my own stuff    all I wanted
someone to do – leave me to grieve and fix the loo!
Chthonic metaphysic!   No shit!  It's enough
mucus of the heart, matter of the mind!

Would it have helped knowing it
was all a story as ancient as ever? I forgot.
I didn't know. I still had to live it.
I still had to have it all crushed out.
I still had to find women to turn to, to laugh about it.
Minus twenty; real feel minus thirty. Real feel falling away feel it!
In her kitchen warmth she gave me *The Gift;* came home with it;
(dark son-in-law you have won me over, won her over, over
there my given daughter in your domain) hell and gone believe it.
Summer here with no rules no walls around it.
No more resistance no more stiffening against it.
May as well shout down the length of an airport
after my disappearing son, like they used to shout
hill to hill at home long ago, drumming right through the night.

2

# Indefiniteness increases suffering
(Kierkegaard)

The first day she reminds me who I am, whatever that means,
it means while she sleeps thirteen hours at a time, fourteen,
I sit on the balcony look up and out at the river, the valley;
from the gift she has brought me *without authority*
I am reading the lily and the bird
   from the world she belongs to, will return to –

threads of fine lines have appeared at her temples
little fissures of awkwardness
   as we stand at the bath where I have brought her
all the clichés of Woolworths' girlieness
(bath salts too sweet, soaps too ribboned, too pink)
to soak off the day and a night and a day's staleness of travel –

we stand  for a moment  together quiet beside the running water
outside the boubou's trembling treble *terribleweeeep terrible weep.*

# Inside

Don't forget how she left the house
with her Hegel, Bob Dylan, the Bible,
full of infection, of flu, prepared nevertheless
for the city, to prepare for her wedding, find the material
for her dress, dresses for her cousins, shoes, a dress
for her mother – last minute lengths
of crazy patterned jersey stretch lacy stuff
instead, to line with taffeta
they found in an old stash
        when they came home –

even the dress was only partly a metaphor:
each little metal button bitten over its silk cover
sending pins and needles all the way up her mother's arm
as when she carried the bride, her first born, inside.

# Giving away

What is the most difficult thing you have done –

re-measured asymmetrical beaded lace appliquéd
on lace, re-boned the underlining, re-cut the cotton
lining machine stitched and hand stitched again each loop in
silk buttonhole stitch across the thread of every loosened loop
over twenty four little covered buttons for keeping
the flexible spine raw silk shadows in folds over ribs breathing
light through the skirt insert lit lace covered godet;

(you can't do it, said the women,
out of that lace – too heavy – there wasn't a pattern –
made the veil anyway with the material's
insistence cut it shorter, cut it into a kind of mantilla);

breath in her breasts   flush under her freckles   all
in the moment concentrated, consecrated.

# Ceremonial

Was it all really only metaphorical, ritual,
like nuptial candles, vows, flowers,
lilies of the field, families,
this, that, his, hers, ours, theirs, ours, our
brothers, brothers-in-law, sisters daughters sons friends
garden paths lights speakers flowers fields
tea tents drinks chairs tables cloths flowers
soup chicken cake cheese fires
suits ties skirts scarves shoes floors;

through the mud in the rain lavatories dragged on a trailer,
the mammoth generator –

when you look back you will see
everything moved itself dance-like
        effortlessly.

# The cake!

The bride could not resist
*beating seventeen eggs! Who can resist!*
With her mother and mother-in-law-to-be
chopping the fruit, talking the ins and outs

of surnames (progeny), and the groom, luckily, with his pedigree,
degree in engineering and brain biology
and now technology and policy,
could work out how to cut the wax wrap – carefully –

and the bride's father grating the rind
and they could all loll around
turning the tins – not to burn – sloshing more brandy –

*easy peasy lemon squeezy* – like the play-list!
sorted by some legend who'd been, gone, come back, luckily
as the bride's brother said (self-effacingly) as MC.

## Confession

Before the wedding
the groom must go to confession –
this his upbringing
requires   what shall I confess
he asks   what is my sin –
six months it takes
before the bride's mother
after a week of intense heat
on an afternoon she can hardly hold
her eyes open   admits
the response   all of it
whatever it is   whatever has held
you from your choice   what you have chosen
all of it  for the life you are given   for giving.

# First words

The bride's grandfather fumbles
when she goes down to greet him
after a long year away *I am going*

*to die* he says "I am going to die"
again as she embraces him –

even when he draws himself back
and up he is no taller –

together on the damp grass
under the bare celtis –

the oak in the field is bare –

what is it? To celebrate
her marriage in the garden
he has kept for her
grandmother, will hurry his day?

# Angry cow

The day before the day before the wedding
the mother of the bride on the road
between the dairy and the bulls
leaves the car running
stands on the hill in the chill
tells her eighty four year old father
to fuck off – why has it taken so long
she follows her weeping daughter
*sophistry* she has heard her eldest brother –
sophists *fuck off* she yells back at her brother
too late! why in the name of need
has she kept denying her own kow-towing
history family story what reason can she concoct
who was not at a wedding why not at what cost.

# Service

*If you want to talk, boy, get down*
*on your knees and talk to God*

he is hissed at, his first service at St Saviour's –
fifty years later in St Boniface in Knysna
from  *Love bade me welcome*  his sister
reads the couple's choice through the reading his daughter
reads  *the leaping deer   the rose of Sharon*
to *the Lord of the Dance*   the last song

through the priest's laughing   giving the sermon
her gravitas   worry not about tomorrow

the bride's mother's eldest brother his mother's

first  the first to come into her room
see   at her temple   the gun
cries   unto the blessing   and the amen.

# The bride cried

at the table, not the awe tears
of walking down the aisle with her father,
they were the twelve years of grief tears,
little motes, little steam wisps. *I miss  Granny;*

her wedding, her grandmother's
garden, and she herself gone as if
impossibly, as if miraculously
she had not chosen it herself

but radiant in the bride's laugh, in the ericas
the uncles, her sons, had gone out and picked,
little bells of pink filling the old milking cans little
varicoloured petals unfolding over the cake; in the cousins,
her grand-daughters, skipping over the grass in the cold,
mud under her tree, where the bride's mother's heels stuck in.

# Swan

Lace like feathers
under the trodden cotton
lining, laced with filaments of grass
and mud at the hem –

when the couple left to go up to the house on the hill
to fetch Fish Hoek Granny's cardboard case, take off the dress –

two small figures in the cold outside the locked back door
she was the only one who saw

(she had wandered from the dancing where she had forgotten
herself – the mother of the bride remembered
they would need the key) as he

possessed with total tenderness
scooped his wife in his jacket over his chest
her silken neck   fallen.

# Bath

As she knelt next to the bath
as she had knelt with her mother
twenty four years before for her new born –
she had to kneel at the edge of the bath
for the full weight to fall
the full length to widen and loosen
the full water to darken
through all the laced and silken folds the cotton
hem! it was only the hem! the underlining
the edge she had thought to rinse
of mud grass and bark-staining tannin
before it could be folded away –
the body of the dress
with its own will   sank in.

# Pools

The mother of the bride, most likely, will always be native
to this place;
the way when the rain comes from the west, middle of the day
she curls like a hedge-hog under the covers the rest of the day;
in the mist listens to the song of frogs;
or when the berg wind gets up at night she can't sleep at all
keeps sniffing the sky   for smoke;
the way these first hot afternoons she does nothing but wait
for snakes;

on a day like this they went down to the rock pools,
the bride and her mother, took off their clothes, thigh deep
the bride swam, and after her dip, from the rocks,
her mother watched   remembered the ancestors  for a moment
washed off their backs.

3

# Mother

These are the years of the dead –
poets, publishers, acquaintances,
friends,   friends' friends,   friends'
relatives, close cousins in car crashes
on the highway past the farm father's sister's son's collision –

something will come   if only   even in a dream
something will come – white bone of death
burning hushed tracks of death grey trunk's ash of death
still flaming black bole of death –   who is to say that even then
something will not come who is to say that death is nothing
even if it is only a dream she may still be, momentarily –

I ask for the sons of the mother of death
to be comforted by her – sons of the dead mother
let her come, even in a dream.

# Daughter

Now that I see
   how in her own life
   she is, in immanence, not about
to be,
   in being
on the other side of the earth
she is
   married to her own life
as only she could be
my daughter –
how could I have loved her
   too closely

how could I ever have loved
   my mother too closely.

## Son

All the time he is going away
further too she tells herself.
as her father's partner tells her
"a daughter always returns".
he will too;
he comes back
for his sister's wedding. he comes back as they say
a changed man;
(all afternoon the washing machine spins
all afternoon the spring wind off the sea)
he shows her the new moon;
everywhere behind his sky-clouded eyes
the soft dark above the river reaches
alive with fire-flies.

# Gradually

 the thicket encroaches;
      grewia, kruisbessie, hardy
      rhus with your  tripartite leafy
indifference   resistance
      thorny, sticky, taaibos;
      sweet camphor of tarconanthus
crushed (who cares you can cry)
      discoloured white green-grey
      bitter little star-apples;
yesterday   already   yearly
even where the hill is grey
the sand is sand even the helichrysum
overgrowing   dying
spikes of needlebush.

# No wonder

my shoulder hurts all the time.
this morning, like most, I limp;
*the Angel in the House*
although they wrestled with her
*"conciliate    conceal    constrict"*

       as if their lives depended on it
       with the strength   of Jacob   at length

       as if there were always enough to risk
       their sons and their daughter
           might not survive it
           in the end

*"useless   what a waste"*

grandmother and mother
took the gun she put in their hands and fired it.

# Tide

Low tide like out breath   wake
with sore neck, stiff back, wrestled all night

like the sea in the dead of night still
out there, talking to itself, continuing, arguing:

the urging sea, the sea urges, breaking itself open urgently
slowly retreats, turns its back: if you don't get up
and do something productive that's your problem –
it's done what it can – it too will lie flat
as if everything were done and said already, already wasted –
again a perfectly boring perfect day what spaces
under your arms as you lie on your back
sea so flat you'd see under the waves little crenellations of sand:

just now the wind will lift a little saying the sea
is starting again sucking at its old sources.

# Teacher

Something new to sweep you away your friends say

*we don't care we don't care we don't care*
she chants when she first opens the door –

you've never met before and she dances light on old feet
her hands take your whole weight –

whatever the details she allows you don't have to repeat

taking the weight way back through the scalp through the spine
fiery old fingers handle the whole thing to lengthen the skeleton

widen the vision   look out look up

*you see   you can be still,*
*I am not doing anything for it.*

Let it live on its own.
Let it speak in its own time.
Let it take up its bones and walk.

# Change

as they say   *you must* – forget the injunction
admonition, interdiction, restriction –   gently, lightly –
don't hold on to the kettle so tightly
as it fills   nor as you pour   out of it –

bend your knees – don't drag the mop across the floor, forget

elbow grease: don't forget: elbows loose at your sides –

revolution, destruction – you can pray – spare me –
you are not, you will not be spared –

but the woman behind the newsreader: look

how she hangs
          her arms loose
          from her shoulders
          only her finger tips
          light on the keys.

# You

Only one thing the teacher asks
look up look out for yourself –

rock martins and white-rumped swifts and little lesser-
striped swallows packing the mud together
again, again letting the wind
                              rip it apart,
little feathered soft breasts, sweethearts!
Find somewhere else, not here where we built!
But they don't, they've got brains as big as birds –

the boubous shriek duet this time *reddy ready poephol ready*

somewhere in the taaibos   secret
as Eleusis  secular as cycles
sacred as days sinking into themselves
*always   only   one   you.*

# Bulls

Blue gold – the days have been –
now they are letting off their marsh smell
mud-stink of vlei-fields, the river mouth open
and draining;
the last of late summer wind hazing everything
and the dogs and I looking for the sun
to lie down
      to walk out in –


seven Angus bulls are lying down in the down-
going sun –
what do they look like – themselves –
stolid, cautiously curious, hirsute, obtuse
and anxious
      we walk past them.

# Who

holds you
　　　　hostage in your own house
boomslang in the entrance
*where do you come from* boomslang
under the jongman's-kas
boomslang under the bed;
all that keeps you from him
sticks　spade　broom　still and dark
*where are you going*
open the door to him
early next day how do you
not tread on him　what
protects you　*what are you*
silence　even the birds have flown.

# Autumn again

Purple still flowering grown over the window
in its own shadow the other window
reflects up to the blind banging down –

where are the harpephyllum seeds, like last year's,
somewhere hidden in its sickle leaves
little red testicle sacs, secrets, if trees had them –

sometimes I think I will die here
if I live here a moment longer –
crazy necky rhus twice bushy tough bostaaibos
close to this talking sea which April is it anyway –

wake to an open sky, far aeroplane,
no-one in the next room,
sometimes I think it will suffocate me this plethora
of plectranthus, vile rhus's ruddy leaves.

# Spring

At home with something out of control
growing like a worm-bark albizia scrappy and stunted
pushing out its pincushion spikes as if it had climbed there,
above the klim-op, that pernicious creeper,

you have come back the same way you went –

it must have been those gums at the Machadadorp toll,
nowhere any emergency services,
the suffocating smog of veld-fire up on the ridge
the corner turned into just as the road took a double track
suddenly smoke so thick
car lights coming towards you almost on top of you
tail lights of the truck in front of you almost invisible
fear of fuck! this must be It –

but all the way to Lydenburg only after-panic sweat.

# Folding

Side-striped jackal grey as just before dawn
hyena sniffing the vast scent
of what has gone what is to come
lion patched with ash basking in black
in mid-day lala palm
retrorse-eared roan share the reservoir;

subtly, subtly   we repeat ourselves like trees
like northern mopanis   tracts   burnt
trunks like chimneys smoking through the whole bole
we die singly   why should we want to be new –
why be afraid
of repeating ourselves –

like folded rhinoceros   we collapse
in what's left   of the shade.

# Now the world takes these breaths

now the world breathes freely
                    now it takes
note  *grant*  gives

fifteen minutes is a long time breathe freely a long time
to have breathed to have taken breath to have
not to have held –

separately   light leaves
police at Kareedouw   paramedics
everyone my son called for help
neighbours, fishermen, the others on the cell phone video
who clambered on the rocks, NSRI,
the brother who had to choose to let go to come out himself,
the body washed up four days on from
Eersterivier to Oubaai.

4

The nightjar is singing again   *here*
*comes the bride*   as if she hadn't come, gone
as if it weren't time for us to go there again –
wherever it is makes us at one again   where
we make ourselves one again with ourselves –
who, what can we blame for making it impossible
how will we get back to that place again
(debt   boredom   apostrophe   parenthesis
half fucking heartedness)
the nightjar gone behind the cloud and the moon
sheepishly, gauchely, like a tall pale child
not wanting to perform at all
(her mask only a mask   everyone knows
from the mark on her neck who she really is).

Morning boubou: *quite untenable* its mate: what *waaiit*
now *terrible* again *horrible*: the jackal buzzard cries like a cat
I hope to god it's got a snake –
mid-day the old man phones, my mouth is full.
*isn't it a bit early* he says *not if you're a poet*
*always hungry* I say and not *alone, grown-up, fifty five:*
*discipline, Joan, discipline* he says and now the boubou
*discipline   terrible   untenable   whaaeet ....*

but only when I lie in my bed way after eight
breakfasting, drinking tea, watching the sky, swifts, rock-martins,
swallows, trying to remember then trying to forget
how dark as night it was in my dream though in my dream
it was only afternoon. I still can't make out the middle syllable
*miracle*   swallow   *miracle   mercy   me   meee?*

Here the water sprays way into beyond
the combretum glaring new green
hiding the boubou insisting this time
*Lucy! Lucy! Oui! Oui –*

maybe my son knows why it's speaking in French –
beautiful young women of the past
don't grieve, maybe a young man you haven't yet seen
even now is driving the city's still streets
under the obdurate spine of the mountain
even a late-middle-aged woman learns to let go
as from Signal Hill to Lion's Head
the whole beast rests;

not so much that I've wasted my life but that it unfolds,
discloses itself like the sun again laid out across my lap.

Once I said what irritates you
about your husband now
will always irritate you but now
even the things that irritate me
I have begun to forget
I suppose this means despite
all my lack of clarity, irritability,
depressiveness, forgetfulness,
what the fuck
we're ok
your father and I even now
with remoteness,
separateness,
rather over-weightiness.

Eventually again in the twenty seventh year of marriage I fell
in love with my husband, maybe I'd fallen before I don't know
I can't remember   it was so slow   nothing happened   we grew
older he worked longer, harder our debt didn't grow smaller;
we didn't see our daughter, our son-in-law, our son came home
once with a group of friends for carrot cake and twice
for four days at a time   we had flu for days, weeks
nothing happened   tragedy came close   scraped by –
one of the friends our son brought home drowned,
mine workers and truck drivers struck, were killed,
the woman who gave the sermon at our daughter's wedding
got her own parish, moved town, got flu, pneumonia, gave in
gave way, our daughter's mother-in-law broke her neck, down
a stairwell, a neck-brace like iron will now drilled to her skull.

Long day – long windy day alone resting my back;

artists, writers in my book fucking one another
like fishes or frogs – amen. So be it. Long windy day – everything
out of control all said discussed like death already – so?
There will be generations, still some with playful tenderness,
inclination to not entirely literalness,
intellectual erotic spiritedness, gayness –

moon rising moon going down,
children out of the fold as if out from under bushes

mists spilling, softening the valleys;

suddenly a jackal as if from nowhere
leaps out in front of the car.

We have talked. We agree. He doesn't want to be left.
I want him to be first so he shows me the way.

Never an October
    you remember
      so still –
then near the middle of the month
    the first thick mist –
      all the frogs in Africa
crammed together
    in chorus;
an accidental moment as you look up,
mid-afternoon's greyness, vagueness,
all at once it's all quite clear –
this is how it is
    it's ok
      it can go.

# Acknowledgements:

Thanks to Colleen Higgs for ALL the work; also to Colleen Crawford Cousins for her thorough engagement in reading and editing. And to Kobus Moolman for being the first careful and encouraging reader.

And to Tammy Griffin for the breathtaking cover image!

# Other Poetry titles by Modjaji Books

The Turtle Dove told Me *by Thandi Sliepen*
Beyond the Delivery Room *by Khadija Heeger*
The Reckless Sleeper *by Haidee Kruger*
Bare & Breaking *by Karin Schimke*
At least the Duck Survived *by Margaret Clough*
removing *by Melissa Butler*
Difficult Gifts *by Dawn Garisch*
Woman Unfolding *by Jenna Mervis*
The Everyday Wife *by Phillippa Yaa de Villiers*
missing *by Beverly Rycroft*
These are the lies I told you *by Kerry Hammerton*
Conduit *by Sarah Frost*
The Suitable Girl *by Michelle McGrane*
Piece Work *by Ingrid Andersen*
Fourth Child *by Megan Hall*
Life in Translation *by Azila Talit Reisenberger*
Please, Take Photographs *by Sindiwe Magona*
Burnt Offering *by Joan Metelerkamp*
Strange Fruit *by Helen Moffett*
Oleander *by Fiona Zerbst*
The Last to Leave *by Maragret Clough*